James Brindley

DERBYSHIRE CANALS

MIKE SMITH
© 1987

Series Editor: Peter J. Naylor

ISBN 0 946404 56 9

Printed and Published by
J. H. Hall & Sons Limited, Siddals Road, Derby
Printers and Stationers since 1831
Telephone: Derby (0332) 45218

THE DERBYSHIRE HERITAGE SERIES

For about sixty years canals were the most important form of transport for heavy goods. They carried raw materials, manufactured goods and foodstuffs more cheaply and more safely than ever before and provided ordinary people with cheaper food and fuel. They linked up the great ports and the main rivers and gave farmers easier access to markets at home and abroad. In Derbyshire, as elsewhere, canals stimulated economic growth and brought increased prosperity.

The Canal Age

The Industrial Revolution burst into life and began to change the face of Britain in the first half of the 18th Century. The development of the factory system by Arkwright and others and the increasing use of steam power, however, created certain problems. Goods began to be manufactured on a much larger scale than under the old domestic system and both raw materials, including coal to power machinery, and manufactured goods needed to be transported over much greater distances.

Unfortunately, road transport by packhorse or wagon was generally slow, costly and sometimes unreliable. Even the building of turnpike roads did not solve the problem since there was no national system of such roads. Furthermore the load which could be pulled or carried by a horse meant that the transportation of heavy or bulky goods remained extremely costly.

The answer to this problem was found when the cotton mill owners, pottery manufacturers, ironmasters and coal owners of this country began to promote the construction of a network of canals throughout the nation.

The first modern canal was the Sankey Brook (St. Helens), partly opened in 1757 to carry coal from St. Helen's coalfield to the Mersey and thence up to the Weaver to the salt industry located there. The Canal Age, however, really began in 1759 with the building of the Duke of Bridgewater's Canal from Worsley Colliery to Manchester. The Duke, who had probably seen the continental canals in the course of a Grand Tour as well as the Sankey Brook nearer home, financed the canal himself and employed as his engineer the famous James Brindley. The completed canal, opened in 1761, cut transportation costs almost by half and made the Duke of Bridgewater a very rich man.

James Brindley ———————— The Duke of Bridgewater

Before long others realised the practical value of canals and the 1770's saw the construction of a number of trunk routes, including the Trent and Mersey, which passes through South Derbyshire for some of its length.

The Canal network in Derbyshire began with the construction of the Trent and Mersey, and Chesterfield canals, both surveyed by James Brindley and both completed in 1777. These were followed over the next twenty years by the Erewash, Peak Forest, Cromford, Nutbrook and Derby Canals.

Before the work of building any canal could begin, however, two important matters had to be dealt with. Money for the project had to be raised and a private Act of Parliament obtained.

It was usual for the promoters of a canal to place advertisements in local newspapers stating the advantages of the proposed navigation and calling on all those interested to attend a meeting. At this meeting a committee would be formed, a subscription list opened and an engineer appointed to survey the route and prepare an estimate of the cost.

Many of the most famous canal engineers had connections with Derbyshire. James Brindley, 'the father of the English canal system' was born in the village of Tunstead in Derbyshire. William Jessop and Benjamin Outram were partners in the Butterley Company.

With the route agreed the next step was to petition parliament for permission to introduce a Bill. The promoters had to persuade as many people as possible to sign petitions to Parliament and sometimes fight off rival schemes. If leave was given to introduce such a Bill the campaign of lobbying and pamphleteering would probably be intensified. The bill would be dealt with by a parliamentary committee but if approved an Act of Parliament would eventually be passed stating details of the proposed route and giving the canal company rights to buy land and obtain water. The Act also protected the rights of those who might lose by the construction of the canal.

The finance for canals came largely from local people who were likely to benefit from the scheme and included Colliery and factory owners, merchants and tradesmen as well as important landowners and the wealthier clergy. Those interested bought shares, which were usually sold in units of £100. Priority in the allocation of shares was given to the original promoters of the scheme.

The canals were dug by gangs of labourers. They were rough and uncouth men who lived by their strength and settled their arguments with their fists, boots and cudgels. Because they were building waterways for boats to navigate these men came to be called navigators or 'navvies'. Specialist craftsmen such as stonecutters, bricklayers and carpenters were also employed to help in the construction of locks, tunnels, bridges and buildings. The work was directed by a Superintendant of Works and usually overseen by the Engineer who drew up the original plans for the canal.

After several years of digging, tunnelling, bridge-building and lock making, the canal would be opened, usually with some ceremony.

Canal companies obtained their revenue from tolls charged to boat owners. Charges were lowest for bulk commodities such as coal and limestone; higher for more valuable bulk cargoes such as iron ore and higher still for finished goods.

For about sixty years canals were the most important form of transport for heavy goods. They carried raw materials, manufactured goods and foodstuffs more cheaply and more safely than ever before and provided ordinary people with cheaper food and fuel. They linked up the great ports and the main rivers and gave farmers easier access to markets at home and abroad.

In Derbyshire, as elsewhere, canals stimulated economic growth and brought increased prosperity. The story of the Derbyshire Canals and of the men who promoted and built them is told in the following chapters.

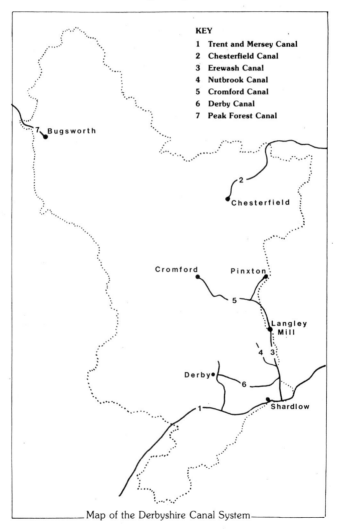

KEY
1 Trent and Mersey Canal
2 Chesterfield Canal
3 Erewash Canal
4 Nutbrook Canal
5 Cromford Canal
6 Derby Canal
7 Peak Forest Canal

Map of the Derbyshire Canal System

The Trent and Mersey Canal and the inland port of Shardlow

The Trent and Mersey was one of the first major canals to be constructed in this country. As early as 1755 the corporation of Liverpool had engaged a surveyor to plan a route from the Trent to either the Mersey or the Weaver. Nothing came of this plan but ten years later the idea was revived. The main inspiration came from Francis Egerton, the third Duke of Bridgewater, who wanted the canal's western terminus to be a junction with his canal (the Bridgewater Canal) at Preston Brook. A rival scheme was promoted by the Trustees of the Weaver Navigation, who wanted the canal to terminate at its western end in the Weaver at Northwich.

Industrialists, led by Josiah Wedgwood and encouraged by Erasmus Darwin, the Derby scientist and philosopher, promoted the idea of a canal politically and finally accepted the Duke of Bridgewater's scheme which had already been surveyed by James Brindley.

On 15th January 1766 a petition for the Trent and Mersey Canal was presented to the House of Commons by landowners, tradesmen and manufacturers in the counties of Lancashire, Cheshire, Staffordshire, Warwickshire, Derbyshire, Leicestershire, Nottinghamshire, Lincolnshire, and Yorkshire. Leave to bring in a bill was requested and the petition was referred to a parliamentary committee.

James Brindley, Josiah Wedgwood and Thomas Bentley (a partner of Wedgwood's) all gave evidence to the committee. Brindley stated that the proposed canal would 'greatly reduce the price of carriage'. Josiah Wedgwood referred to the large manufactures in the neighbourhood of the intended canal, particularly a great pottery near Newcastle-under-Lyme. The raw materials and manufactured goods of that pottery

The Lock House at Shardlow

amounted to 10,000 or 12,000 tons per annum; and the canal would reduce the expense of carriage for these by three-quarters. Thomas Bentley gave further examples of the economies which the canal would produce and John Sparrow (a lawyer from Newcastle-under-Lyme) informed the committee that £63,000 had already been subscribed towards the canal, and stated he was confident that the whole sum could easily be obtained. Convinced by these arguments the committee gave leave for a bill to be brought in.

Petitions and pamphlets for and against the Trent and Mersey were numerous but the promoters won the day and the Trent and Mersey Canal bill received the Royal Assent on 14th May 1766. The preamble of the Act outlined the course of the canal 'from the R. Trent, near Wilden bridge, below an ancient ferry called Wilden Ferry, to the R. Mersey, at or near a certain place called Runcorn Gap'.

The first meeting of the company of proprietors of the canal was held on the 10th June 1766 when a number of appointments were made. John Sparrow was appointed clerk at a salary of £100 per annum; James Brindley as surveyor general was given a salary of £150 per annum; and Hugh Henshall as clerk of the works had a salary of £150 per annum for himself and one clerk. Josiah Wedgwood was elected honorary treasurer and a call of £6 per cent was ordered to be made upon subscribers. Work was ordered to be begun at both ends of the Harecastle tunnel and at Wilden Ferry.

Construction began officially on 26th July 1766 when the first sod was ceremonially cut by Josiah Wedgwood. Other local worthies cut a turf or wheeled a barrow to commemorate the event and in the afternoon a sheep was roasted in Burslem market place. Work proceeded well and at the General Assembly of the proprietors held on 29th September 1768 it was reported that 22 miles of the navigation had been completed; 14 locks, 26 bridges and six boats had been built; and that '409 yards of the subterraneous Passage at Harecastle are cut and vaulted, besides the vast Openings at each Entrance'. By April 1773 it was reported that 66 miles of the navigation were 'entirely finished' and that the canal from Wilden Ferry to Stoke had been navigable 'for some time' and that 'many vessels' had used it.

The canal was finally completed in May 1777, but unusually the occasion was not commemorated with any lavish celebration.

For much of its life the canal was a considerable commercial

A typical warehouse, probably the best preserved and least altered building in Shardlow

and financial success. Goods such as coal, iron ore, stone, flint, clay, lime, pottery, salt, corn, cheese and timber were all transported along the canal. In addition, from the ports, came such items as beer, wine, tobacco, sugar and cotton. Nor was traffic confined to long distance hauls. The canal served the many small communities along its length in a variety of ways.

This commercial success led of course to considerable financial gain for the shareholders. After the completion of construction work and the paying of debts the dividends began to increase substantially. As a result shares soon began to change hands at a considerable premium. In 1806 the £100 shares were selling at £840 and the annual dividend was 40 per cent. Between 1820 and 1831 the annual dividend reached a phenomenal 75 per cent!

What, however, was the place of Shardlow in this enterprise? Shardlow was chosen by Brindley to be the transhipment point where goods were transferred from the narrow boats which operated on the canal, to the larger barges which navigated the River Trent. As this transhipment was not usually from boat to boat, warehouses had to be built to store the goods until they were needed for the onward journey. In the area between the canal and the turnpike road to Derby (now the A6) a large number of impressive brick-built warehouses were constructed. Basins and inlets were excavated to give access to these warehouses and wharfs were built to accommodate the hundreds of boats which unloaded their cargoes. In addition to a number of general warehouses two iron warehouses and two salt warehouses were built here. Trade was so brisk that three firms trading in bulk goods maintained agents in Shardlow: Corte & Co., paper dealers of Leicester; Shipton & Co., timber merchants of Wolverhampton; and Daniel & Company, iron merchants of London.

The port of Shardlow dealt with a wide variety of goods including coal, iron, limestone, gypsum, bar iron, salt, lead, pottery, ale, cheese, timber, malt and barley, and boats returned to Shardlow with cotton from Manchester which was transported to the Trent and sent to Nottingham. So busy did this little settlement become that it was known locally as 'Little Liverpool' or 'a rural Rotterdam'.

The Lady in Grey dates from 1790 and was formerly the home of the Soresby family

After 1811 boats conveyed goods from Shardlow to Derby, Market Harborough, Hull, Sleaford, Loughborough, Leicester, Nottingham, Grantham, Lincoln, Newark, Boston, Gainsborough, Horncastle, Manchester and Melton Mowbray, and to all places on the line of the Trent and Mersey and Bridgewater Canals.

These boats were hauled by horses and at one time Shardlow had stabling for over 100 horses.

The coming of the canal brought new industries in its wake including malting, brewing, boat building, rope making and corn milling and the population rose from around 300 in 1789 to 1,306 in 1841. This 'golden age' was short lived however, for with the coming of the railways Shardlow began to decline in importance and prosperity. In 1846 the Trent and Mersey Canal Company was itself amalgamated with the North Staffordshire Railway Company and although this canal fared better in the hands of a railway company than many others the heyday of the canal was over. Many of the warehouses were diverted to other uses as traffic gradually declined.

Commercial traffic did, however, continue until well after the Second World War. The last load of grain was delivered as late as 1951 and newsprint for the Derby newspapers was

Mile post at Shardlow

carried from Hull to the British Waterways Wharf at Cavendish Bridge until the early 1950's.

The Shardlow story has a happy ending however. In 1975 the Shardlow Wharf Conservation Area was created and many of the buildings that served the canal are now 'listed' as worthy of preservation for historical or architectural reasons. Many have been restored to their former glory or converted to other uses and the village stands today as probably the best example of an 18th century inland port surviving in this country.

The Clock Warehouse, Shardlow

The Chesterfield Canal

The Chesterfield Canal was an early yet ambitious venture designed to link Chesterfield with the Trent. It was promoted by a number of interests including: the Cavendish family who owned a furnace and a forge at Staveley, the London Lead Company who wanted a more convenient shipping place than Bawtry for the products of their smelt mill at Ashover and several important local landowners who wished to exploit their coal resources.

James Brindley was engaged to make a survey and prepare plans and estimates. Reporting to a public meeting held at Worksop on 24th August 1769, he proposed a route running from Chesterfield to Northwood, past Shireoaks and Worksop to East Retford and thence to the Trent at West Stockwith.

The meeting decided to apply for an Act of Parliament to build the canal and despite opposition from the River Don Company the Act'. . . for making a navigable Cut or Canal from Chesterfield, in the County of Derby, through or near Worksop and Retford, to join the River Trent, at or near Stockwith, in the county of Nottingham' received the Royal

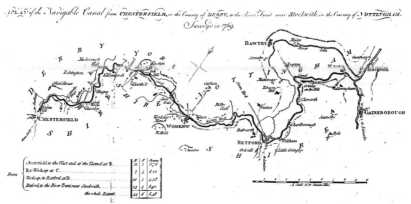

Plan of the navigable canal from Chesterfield in the County of Derby to the River Trent, near Stockwith in the County of Nottingham, surveyed in 1769

Assent on March 28th 1771. When the news reached Chesterfield bells were rung in the churches and fireworks were let off in the market place.

The Act gave powers to raise £100,000 in £100 shares and £50,000 more if necessary. Subsciption lists were opened both locally and in London and within a few months the capital was fully subscribed. Investors in the project included Brindley himself who held 15 shares, substantial landowners such as the Dukes of Devonshire, Newcastle and Leeds, and lead merchants such as the Twiggs of Ashover and Chesterfield, Allwood Wilkinson of Chesterfield and William Milnes of Ashover. They were joined in the enterprise by several iron founders and dealers as well as a number of local tradesmen, gentlemen, physicians and clergymen, some of whom held only one or two shares.

James Brindley was engaged at a salary of £300 per annum for 'superintending the Execution of the works . . . until the same shall be completed'. As Brindley could only give part of his time to the project the committee appointed John Varley

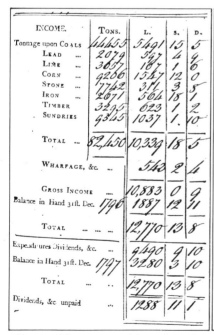

Abstract of the income and expenditure for the Chesterfield Canal for the year 1797

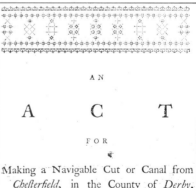

Act of Parliament authorising the Chesterfield Canal

(Brindley's pupil) as Clerk of the Works at a salary of £100 per annum.

At a meeting of the Proprietors held at Harthill in June 1771 Brindley outlined his plans. The first operation was to complete the tunnel through the magnesian limestone ridge at Norwood in two years and then to open up the section of the canal from the east of the tunnel to Shireoaks. He estimated that the whole canal would be complete in four years.

Teams of navvies were recruited to carry out the work. The committee was obviously aware of the reputation such men had for drunkenness and violence for they ordered that: ·

'. . . if any wilful mischief or Damage shall be done to any Person or Persons whatsoever by any of the Workmen employed in the works of the said navigation that such workmen will be immediately discharged from the Works and that they will be prosecuted for the offence by them committed at the Expense of the Company . . .'

The supervision of such a large group of labourers was a difficult task and it became necessary to employ tally-men to patrol the works and make checks for absenteeism. The minute book of the canal company records that 'John Best be allowed Twelve Shillings per week for counting the men employed at the works twice every day'.

Work proceeded well at first. Construction started at Norwood in October 1771 and in the following February the Committee ordered Varley to stake out the line of the canal from Norwood to Worksop. In May he was instructed to continue it as far as Retford.

Brindley died in the Autumn of 1772 and John Varley was appointed Resident Engineer. At the same time Hugh Henshall was engaged to make a survey every three months and attend when required. Towards the end of 1773, however, it was discovered that Varley had been giving contracts to his family at inflated prices and passing poor workmanship. The minutes of the Committee for 12th May 1774 record that '. . . several lettings or bargains have been imprudently made at prices greatly exceeding the real value thereof and in a collusive manner'.

He was compelled to enter into a bond of £500 and his

relatives were discharged. Hugh Henshall was appointed Chief Engineer and although Varley was retained he was required in future to be, 'well behaving and demeaning himself in the Duties of his office as Clerk of the Works'.

The company also faced financial problems which slowed down construction but the canal was eventually completed in June 1777. The Derby Mercury for 6-13th June published the following report of the opening ceremonies:

'As Canal Navigations have ever been found highly beneficial to the Public especially to those concerned in Trade; it is with very great pleasure that we inform our Readers that the Canal from Chesterfield to Stockwith is now navigable from one end to the other, and we hear from Chesterfield, that a boat laden with goods from Stockwith, was brought to that town on Wednesday last (being the King's Birthday), when the Canal there was opened; — an event so long wished for, so interesting and advantageous, could not be regarded as a common occurence, and therefore was celebrated by the Proprietors of the Town, and the Inhabitants in general with all those demonstations of satisfaction and joy, which they must feel upon such an occasion. The boat was met at the first lock by several gentlemen of the committee and a great number of the proprietors, attended by a very large concourse of people, and was introduced, with colours flying, firing of guns, and a band of music, after which the goods were unloaded and put into waggons, which were drawn to the town by the navigators, proceeded by the gentlemen of the committee and the proprietors, who walked in procession with the music playing before them. The assiduity of the workmen, whose labour for the last three weeks, almost exceeds belief, was rewarded by a handsome treat given them by the proprietors, of which near 300 of them partook, and the gentlemen of the town concluded the day over a cheerful glass; the ringing of the bells, bonfires and fireworks contributing to the festivity of the evening. We cannot help mentioning one circumstance to the honour of the poor working navigators, who tho' generally stiled the Sons of Riot and Confusion, behaved in the most decent and orderly manner, and dispersed early in the evening, without making any disturbance whatever.

The next day, the gentlemen gave the ladies a treat upon the water, and the boat which was honoured with bringing the first load of goods to Chesterfield, received the additional and much greater honour of conveying above 100 ladies of that town through the first lock; the boat was lined and decorated with streamers and furnished with an excellent band of music provided for the occasion'.

One immediate result of the opening of the canal was that the price of coal at East Retford dropped from 15s.6d. (77½p) to 10s.6d. (52½p) a ton. In other respects, however, the canal was not an immediate success. During construction the

Fellows, Morton and Clayton warehouse on the Chesterfield Canal at Worksop

canal had run into financial difficulties which slowed the work down. An attempt was made to raise additional calls on the shares but when this failed £53,000 had to be borrowed. As a result a high proportion of the trading profits had to be paid out in interest charges. To make matters worse traffic failed to develop as quickly as had been anticipated and in 1782 the proprietors attempted to lease the canal. This move proved to be unsuccessful as there were no takers but traffic began to increase with the construction of horse-drawn tramways to collieries at Inkersall, Spinkhill, Norbriggs and Glasshouse Common.

The first dividend, a mere one per cent, was paid to shareholders in 1789. The traffic for that year comprised: 42,379 tons of coal, 7,569 tons of stone, 4,366 tons of corn, 3,955 tons of lime, 3,862 tons of lead and 1,544 tons of iron together with much smaller quantities of pottery, ale and other sundry items. By 1795 the company was able to pay a dividend of 6% and a modest prosperity was maintained until the middle of the 19th century.

In addition to the regular cargoes already mentioned the Chesterfield Canal also played its part in the history of our nation. During the Napoleonic Wars armaments manufactured in and around Chesterfield were taken by canal boats to West Stockwith and from there by river to Hull where they were transferred to waiting ships for speedy passage to our armies in Europe. Early in 1840 the first cargo of Anston stone for the new Houses of Parliament was carried on the canal to West Stockwith for transhipment. Approximately 250,000 tons were transported in total.

Tonnage reached a peak in 1848 when 201,544 tons of goods were carried. By this time, however, the canal had already been taken over by the Manchester, Sheffield and Lincolnshire Railway and within ten years the amount carried had fallen to only 110,761 tons.

In 1871 the first effects of mining subsidence were felt at the Norwood Tunnel and although £21,000 was spent on repairs over the next 35 years the Royal Commission of 1906 reported that only 40 boats were working on the canal and none beyond the tunnel on the Chesterfield side. In 1908 part of the tunnel finally collapsed bringing an end to almost all the

Turnerwood Basin on the Chesterfield Canal

traffic above Shireoaks. The last commercial traffic was from the brickyards at Walkeringham to West Stockwith and this finally ceased in 1955. Within a few years the canal had became derelict and largely unpassable. Fortunately, this decline was halted and reversed. In 1961 the canal was saved from abandonment by a group of enthusiasts and it is today navigable between West Stockwith and Worksop.

THE EREWASH AND NUTBROOK CANALS

Coal stimulated the building of both the Erewash and Nutbrook canals. It had been mined for centuries in the Erewash Valley and was sold both locally and in adjacent parts of Nottinghamshire. The opening of the Loughborough Navigation however, expanded the market for the coal trade in Southern Leicestershire and led to the need for improved transport along the Erewash Valley.

Shortly after work had begun on the Loughborough Navigation some of its supporters combined with colliery owners, businessmen and landowners in Derbyshire and Nottinghamshire to promote the Erewash Canal. On their behalf a certain John Smith surveyed a line 11¾ miles long from the River Trent below Sawley to Langley Mill.

These men acted swiftly. Public meetings were held in Heanor and Nottingham in November and December 1776 and the Act authorising the Canal was carried on second reading in the House of Commons on 30th April 1777.

The company was empowered to raise £15,400 in £100 shares and £7,700 more if necessary. Over half these subscriptions came from people living in Leicestershire and a close working relationship was maintained with the Loughborough Navigation Company. At the first meeting of the Erewash Company William Craddock, a Loughborough attorney who was already Clerk and Treasurer to the Loughborough Navigation, was appointed to the same combined offices of the Erewash Canal Company. This relationship was further strengthened by the fact that the management committee of seven contained two members of the Loughborough Navigation Committee and two others connected with the navigation.

Trent Lock, the entrance to the Erewash Canal

John Varley, who at one time had been apprenticed to James Brindley and was Clerk of Works on the Chesterfield canal, was appointed Engineer at a salary of £220 per annum. The canal was built under contract by James and John Pinkerton of North Cave in the East Riding of Yorkshire. They began work almost immediately and with few topographical difficulties to be faced, progress was rapid.

Water was let into the lower part of the canal and tolls were collected from 24th October 1778. By 30th April in the following year the canal was navigable from Trent Lock to the coal pits near Ilkeston Common and by about July for its full length as far as Langley Mill.

The canal was officially opened on 10th December 1779 when, according to the local press, a 'grand regatta' was held to celebrate the occasion. The proprietors travelled along the canal in a 'handsomely decorated' barge displaying 'the most lively colours'. Muskets and small cannon were let off as they passed each bridge and coal wharf and thousands watched as they slowly made their way to the terminus of the canal at Langley Mill. Here they disembarked and marched off to dinner led by a band and accompanied by the contractors and their workmen.

A few engineering works remained to be completed after the official opening but by this time John Varley found himself in trouble once again. He had failed to keep proper accounts for land and damage compensation payments and had also made a mistake in the levels of the uppermost lock. He was dismissed as engineer in May 1780 and in August the lock had to be taken down and rebuilt. Varley was ordered to pay the cost of £78 less the value of the bricks but there is no record of whether or not he complied.

The anticipated coal trade was slow to develop and the following notice appeared in the Derby Mercury on 12th September 1782:

"NAVIGATION

Notice is hereby GIVEN, by the Proprietors of the Erewash Canal, to such Gentlemen as have Collierys near the Line of the said Canal, that there is and has been cause of Complaint of the great Scarcity of COALS, to supply the Consumption wanted upon the said Canal; they earnestly recommend to such Gentlemen as have COALS upon the Line of the said Canal to open Pits and the said Proprietors engage to allow every Conveniency to such new Pits, as they have already done to those of the old One's"

Pits were opened and within a few years a network of tramways had been constructed to bring coal to the many wharves along the line of the canal. In 1792 the canal carried 70,000 tons of coal and with the opening of the Cromford, Derby and Nutbrook canals this had increased to 270,000 by 1808. Other goods were of course carried on the canal including limestone, lead, iron, millstones, chalk and marble.

This growth in trade brought prosperity for the shareholders. The first dividend of 2½ per cent for the year 1783 had risen to 20 per cent by 1787 and 30 per cent by 1794. In 1826 dividends rose to an amazing peak of 74 per cent and six years later the £100 shares had a market value of £1,300 each.

The Erewash Canal at Sandiacre

The value of these shares fell rapidly, however, with the growth of railway competition. In 1834 the Leicester and Swannington Railway was completed, giving access to all the coal Leicester needed at a far cheaper rate than ever before. In 1847 the Erewash Valley Railway was opened between Long Eaton and Codnor Park and branch lines were soon built to serve a number of collieries which had previously shipped their coal by canal.

Despite reductions in tolls, traffic declined rapidly and by the 1860's all that remained was some through traffic from other canals and the coal brought by rail to the Long Eaton basin to be transhipped for the short journey down the canal and then on to the Trent. This decline continued into the next century until 1932 when the canal was purchased by the Grand Junction Railway Company. Some coal traffic was brought on to the canal but the Nottingham and Cromford Canals were by this time impassable and it was not possible to reverse years of decline and neglect. Traffic had virtually ceased by the end of the Second World War and nationalisation in 1947 did nothing to revive the fortunes of the Erewash Canal.

Closure came in 1968 when the Transport Act of that year

defined it as a 'remainder waterway'. To prevent it becoming derelict the Erewash Canal Preservation and Development Association was formed. Thanks to the hard work of these enthusiasts the county councils of Derbyshire and Nottinghamshire were persuaded to finance the restoration of the canal to cruising standard and in 1973 the E.C.P.D.A. itself completed restoration of the Great Northern Basin at Langley Mill.

Traditional narrow boats moored at the Great Northern Basin,
Langley Mill during a rally in 1986

The Nutbrook Canal

The Nutbrook Canal was built as an independent branch of the Erewash Canal for the purpose of serving the West Hallam and Shipley collieries. It carried little but coal, iron and limestone and was only 4½ miles long. Isolated from the main lines of communication it was important only to the industries that it directly served. Nevertheless, it played its own small part in the economic development of Derbyshire and is worthy of at least a footnote.

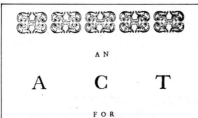

AN

A   C   T

FOR

Making and Maintaining a Navigable Canal from the Collieries at *Shipley* and *Weſthallam*, in the County of *Derby*, to the *Erewaſh* Canal, in the Pariſh of *Stanton by Dale*, in the ſaid County.

WHEREAS the making and maintaining a Navigable Canal from certain Coal Mines called *Shipley* and *Weſthallam* Collieries, in the County of *Derby*, to join and communicate with a certain Navigable Canal, made in purſuance of an Act of Parliament of the Seventeenth Year of the Reign of His preſent Majeſty, called "The *Erewaſh* Canal," in the Pariſh of *Stanton by Dale*, in the ſaid County, being about the Diſtance of Five Miles, will be of public Utility:

And whereas Sir *Henry Hunloke*, Baronet, is Owner of the ſaid *Weſthallam* Colliery, and *Edward Miller Mundy*, Eſquire, is Owner of the ſaid *Shipley* Colliery:

And whereas the ſaid Sir *Henry Hunloke* and the ſaid *Edward Miller Mundy* are willing and deſirous to undertake to make and maintain ſuch Navigable Canal as aforeſaid: But the ſame cannot be effected without the Authority of Parliament;

Act of Parliament authorising the Nutbrook Canal

The Nutbrook Canal was promoted by Edward Miller-Mundy of Shipley Hall, the owner of collieries at Shipley, and Sir Henry Hunloke of Wingerworth, near Chesterfield, the owner of the estate and collieries at West Hallam. The Act authorising the canal was passed in June 1793 and the Munday family became the largest shareholder by taking up 41 of the 130 shares issued.

The canal was built by direct labour under the direction of Benjamin Outram. He was retained for a fee of £200 and promised a bonus of £50 if he finished the work before the beginning of 1795. It was, however, a bonus which he failed to collect for the canal was not completed until 1796 and cost more than originally estimated.

Traffic in coal from the Shipley and West Hallam collieries built up rapidly and within ten years about fifty thousand tons per year were being carried. This had risen to a peak of 126,786 tons in 1853-4. Like other canals in the area, however, the Nutbrook Canal was affected by railway competition. The building of branch lines from the Erewash Valley Railway to the Nutbrook and Shipley collieries resulted in a decline in traffic and the canal also suffered from mining subsidence.

Traffic eventually ceased in 1895 although the lower part of the canal was used until as late as 1947 by the Stanton Ironworks Company. Since that time much of the line has been obliterated and it is now virtually impossible to trace the route that it once took.

The Cromford Canal

Cromford is well known as the birthplace of the factory system for it was here in 1771 that Richard Arkwright established the world's first successful water-powered cotton spinning mill. Within a few years a complex of mills had been constructed as well as offices, warehouses, a hotel and substantial housing for the mill workers and their families.

Communications around Cromford were, however, poor. The carriage of raw cotton from Lancashire to Cromford was particularly difficult and the movement of both raw materials and finished goods in and out of the area involved arduous and expensive road journeys by packhorse or wagon.

It was not cotton though but coal which first encouraged the promotion of the Cromford Canal. The waterway which eventually became the Cromford Canal was first suggested by a group of landowners in the Erewash valley. In letters to the Erewash Canal Company, written in 1787, they urged an extension of the Erewash Canal upwards towards Pinxton arguing that a six mile stretch of coal on the Erewash was unworked 'owing to a lack of communication'. In July of that year a group of these men, together with Benjamin Outram and John Hodgkinson (Outram's associate) met the Erewash proprietors. This meeting came to nothing but in the following year Sir Richard Arkwright took a hand. With a group of business associates he decided to pursue the idea of a navigation to connect the mills at Cromford with the terminal basin of the Erewash Canal at Langley Mill. William Jessop was engaged to prepare plans and an estimate of the cost.

Arkwright's group included the Gells and the Beresfords, Benjamin Outram, the Jessops and the Hodgkinsons, who were Outram's in-laws. These men represented interests in iron, coal, limestone, lead and cotton. The advantage of a canal connecting Cromford with the Trent with the textile

Bridge over the canal near Cromford

districts around Nottingham and with the two major ports of Liverpool and Hull was obvious to them. It is not surprising therefore that when Jessop submitted his plan and an estimate of £42,697 in December 1788, half of this sum was raised immediately, and the rest within two weeks.

The share capital of the company was £46,000 divided into 460 shares of £100 held by 78 shareholders. A small committee was elected of which Sir Richard Arkwright was chairman.

The Cromford Canal was authorised by Parliament in the following year despite opposition from Jedediah Strutt and Thomas Evans, who feared a distortion of water suplies to their mills at Belper, Milford and Darley Abbey, lower down the Derwent. The canal was to run from Cromford to Langley Mill with a two mile branch from Ironville to Pinxton.

Jessop and Outram were appointed engineers to the company. Jessop received £350 per annum and expenses for giving one third of his time to the works and Outram was engaged as his full time assistant, at a salary of £200. The project was divided into three contracts totalling £37,113.3s.6d., awarded to Thomas Skeasley of Tamworth and Thomas Roundford of Coleridge in Staffordshire, who undertook to construct the Pinxton arm and the branch to the eastern end of the deep cutting at Butterley in eighteen months, the section from the western end of the deep cutting to Cromford in two years and the tunnel at Butterley in three. Before long, however, it became obvious that the canal could not be constructed for the contract price as the cost of land, labour and materials had all increased due to wartime inflation. In January 1791 the contractors absconded and the two engineers took over the work by direct labour; Outrams salary being increased to £400.

By the time of the Annual Meeting in May 1792 it was clear that the original share capital would be insufficient to complete construction. Shareholders had to contribute an additional £35 on each share and the sum of £9,300 was raised on mortgage secured to the tolls to be levied by the company. When even this proved to be insufficient a short term loan of £2,000 was obtained from Mr. Francis Beresford.

There were problems also with construction. Early in 1792 the Bull Bridge Aqueduct began to crack apart and had to be repaired. In 1793 cracks also appeared in the Wigwell Aqueduct spanning the Derwent. In both cases Jessop accepted the blame and offered to meet the cost of restoration himself, declaring, "Painfull as it is to me to lose the good opinions of my friends, I would receive their censure for the faults of my head rather than of my heart".

The canal was eventually opened in August 1794 at a cost of nearly twice Jessop's original estimate.

Despite these early problems the Cromford Canal was destined to be one of the success stories of the early industrial era. It widened the scope of the markets available to the coal and mineral owners and the manufacturers in the area; it cheapened the price of fuel and other necessities to the inhabitants of mid-Derbyshire and it was a financial success bringing handsome rewards to its shareholders.

Coal, limestone and ironstone were important cargoes and a large number of tramroads were built to connect collieries, limestone quarries and ironstone workings to the many wharfs on the canal. In the Riddings area asses were used for hauling wagons along these tramways; in Swanwick and Birchwood district steam whimsies were in use. Other important collieries lay close to the canal in the Langley Mill area and tramways and wharves were built here also. By these means considerable quantities of local coal were carried by canal into Leicestershire and the lower Trent Valley.

Apart from coal and coke, which consistantly provided for over seventy-five per cent of its trade the canal was also used for transporting a wide variety of raw materials and manufactured goods. It served Arkwright's cotton mills by transporting both raw cotton and textile yarn; chert was conveyed from Bakewell to the Potteries and building stone from local quarries was carried throughout the country.

The Butterley Company made substantial use of the canal. Two shafts were sunk into the Butterley Tunnel from the Iron-

Leawood Pump House

works yard and goods were lowered to and from the barges below by whimsies. During the early years of the 19th century the company was engaged in making cannon and shot for use in the war against Napoleon and this was carried by waterway to Woolwich Arsenal. For many years the canal carried limestone from Crich to serve as a flux in the Butterley furnaces and the wide range of products manufactured by the company were carried by waterway throughout the Kingdom.

For a number of years the firm of Nathaniel Wheatcroft, based at Cromford Wharf operated a passenger service between Cromford and Nottingham, a distance of 38 miles. Canal boats were also used on occasions for Sunday School 'treats' and similar excursions when a working narrow boat might be specially cleaned and decorated.

For many years the Cromford Canal was a very profitable enterprise. From 1804 until the company was sold in 1852 it never paid less than 10% to its shareholders, and for seven years, from 1835, it paid 20% or more with a maximum of 28% in 1841. This financial success was reflected in the price of shares which had a market value of £550 in 1824.

There were, however, some difficulties in the operation of the canal. The locks at the eastern end were wide and could accommodate boats up to fourteen feet in beam so that the Erewash Canal boats could navigate as far as the eastern end of the Butterley Tunnel. The tunnel though was narrow and navigation through to Cromford was only possible to narrow boats of some seven foot beam. To make matters worse this section of the canal was shallower than normal so that Cromford Canal boats were only of some thirty inches draught and their carrying capacity only about twenty two tons compared with the usual thirty to thirty-five tons.

The long narrow Butterley Tunnel also created problems for the passage of boats along the canal. Limitations were imposed on the movement of traffic and the following notices were placed at the entrances of the tunnel:-

"No boat shall enter the east end of the Butterley Tunnel except between the hours of 5 & 6 o'clock morning & 1 & 2 afternoon and 9 & 10 at night and no boat shall enter the west end of the tunnel except between the hours of 1 & 2 morning and 9 & 10 forenoon and 5 & 6 in the afternoon, and every boat shall make its passage thro' the same with all possible dispatch and on no account exceed 3 hours after entry. And every person having the care of any boat shall offend he or they shall forfeit for every such offence the sum of 20s and shall also turn back upon meeting another boat in the tunnel".

The greatest problem which faced the company, however, was probably a shortage of water and this difficulty reached dramatic proportions in 1844 when two-thirds of the supply from Cromford Sough ceased after the lead mines began to be worked at a lower level. To overcome this problem the Canal Company first hired a pumping engine and later in 1849, installed a beam engine at Leawood to raise water from the Derwent.

The opening of the Cromford and High Peak Railway in 1831 linking Cromford with the Peak Forest Canal at Whaley Bridge brought more traffic on to the canal but before long it had to face competition from the railways. By 1849 it had lost much of its traffic to the Manchester, Buxton, Matlock and Midland Junction Railway and after protracted negotiations the canal was finally sold to this railway company.

There followed a long but gradual period of decline. It was not, however, until 1944 that the canal was finally abandoned as a navigable waterway.

Today the Cromford Canal has a new role as a leisure amenity and many thousands of people enjoy walking the towpath and taking a ride on the horse-drawn barge operated by the Cromford Canal Society.

The Derby Canal

Few people are today aware of the existence of the Derby Canal. This is not really surprising since that part of the canal which ran through the city centre was obliterated by new road schemes; much has been filled in and what does remain has been described as a linear refuse tip. It was, however, in its heyday, a busy and important waterway and Derby was an inland port bigger in extent even than Shardlow.

By the end of the 18th century the rapidly growing town of Derby was in need of improved transportation for industries as varied as textiles, engineering, clock making, china and the production of rolled iron and copper sheeting.

A number of different schemes were suggested to link Derby with the regional canal network but on 30th July

——— Leaflet promoting the intended Derby Canal ———

32

1792 a meeting was held at the Bell Inn at which it was proposed to construct a canal linking Derby with Swarkestone, Smithy Houses, Sandiacre, Shardlow and Swadlincote. A committee was appointed which comprised local landowners, industrialists, bankers and coalmasters as well as representatives of the Derby Navigation Company, the Grand Trunk Company and the Erewash Company.

Benjamin Outram was commissioned to make surveys and a "second opinion" was later sought from William Jessop. The committee finally approved proposals for lines from Derby to Swarkestone (on the Trent and Mersey Canal); to Sandiacre (on the Erewash Canal) and to Little Eaton with a horse-drawn tramway to Smithy Houses. There was no shortage of financial support and only a day after their issue the Derby Mercury reported that shares were changing hands at a premium of £20 upwards.

A vigorous campaign was fought against rivals and objectors and the Derby Canal Bill finally received the Royal Assent on 7th May 1793. A few weeks later the first General Assembly of the Derby Canal Company was held at the Bell Inn in Sadler Gate. A committee was elected to manage the affairs of the company and Benjamin Outram was appointed as engineer.

ANNO TRICESIMO TERTIO

Georgii III. Regis.

C A P. CII.

An Act for making and maintaining a Navigable Canal from the River *Trent*, at or near *Swark-stone Bridge*, to and through the Borough of *Derby* to *Little Eaton*, with a Cut out of the said Canal in or near the said Borough, to join the *Erewash* Canal near *Sandiacre*; and for making Rail Ways from such Canal to several Collieries in the Parishes or Liberties of *Denby*, *Horsley*, and *Smalley*, all in the County of *Derby*.   [7th May 1793.]

WHEREAS the making and maintaining a Canal for the Navigation of Boats, Barges, and other Vessels, from the River Trent, near Swarkstone Bridge, in the Parish of Swarkstone, in the County of Derby, to and through the Liberty of the Borough of Derby, to Little Eaton in the County of Derby, with a Branch or Cut out of the said Canal in or near the said Borough of Derby, to join the Erewash Canal near Sandiacre, in the said Coun-

9   30 I 2   ty;

Derby Canal, Act of Parliament

Rapid progress was made and at a committee meeting held on 6th July 1793 it was reported that work had already commenc-·ed on cutting the canal. It was at this meeting that the officers of the company were officially appointed. Mr. George Wooton was appointed Superintendant of Works at a salary of £150 per annum. His duties were: "to see that all the surveyors are at their places, that materials are provid-ed for each job of work wanted

— to purchase all small matters wanted — to see that all the Iron Work, Timber and other materials are sound and good — to view every part of the lines at least twice a week — to see that proper care is taken of the fences and as little trespass done as possible — to employ Day Men where he shall see necessary and to see their due attention — and to attend to all carriage work".

Mr. William White was appointed book keeper at a salary of £105 per annum and his duties were described as "to admeasure all the cutting according to the Bargains let — the Lawyers work, the stone cutters, Brick layers and Carpenters work — to take from the surveyors accounts of all materials and implements delivered and to whom consigned — to keep a Debtor and Creditor account with every workman and to attend to the pay table — to direct what the treasurer shall pay to each workman and to be responsible for the accounts".

These two men were responsible for supervising most of the day-to-day work of constructing the canal and, as was usual, Mr. Benjamin Outram, the engineer, would make only periodic visits to keep a check on the progress being made and to give advice on particular problems as they arose. Over six hundred navvies were employed together with carpenters, stone-cutters and bricklayers.

Entrance to the Derby Canal at Swarkestone

The canal, when completed in 1796, ran from Swarkestone to Derby and then on to Little Eaton from where a horse-drawn railway ran to Denby. In addition a branch connected Derby with the Erewash Canal at Sandiacre. One of the chief reasons why the canal had been built was to bring coal cheaply to Derby but this was not the only cargo carried. Boats on the Sandiacre line in particular, carried a wide variety of goods. It was along this line that boats coming from the Erewash Canal proceeded, bringing such things as iron, limestone, paving stones and other goods in addition to coal. On the Swarkestone line cargoes included corn, cement, castings, lead and timber. There is little detailed information about the type and extent of goods carried on the canal but the minute book of the company contains the following accounts of tonnage which was entered "by the direction of the committee for future reference".

The Lock and Toll House on the Erewash Canal at the junction with the Derby Canal at Sandiacre. This was used by the Derby Canal Company until 1832 when they built their own toll house (now demolished) on the opposite bank of the Derby Canal

SANDIACRE LINE   FEBRUARY 1839

	Tons	Cwts		£	s.	d.
Corn	3031	10	@ 10d	126	6	3
Coal	1370	10		57	2	2
Sundries	1485	10		61	17	11
Bricks	209	10		8	14	7
Cement	281	10		11	14	7
Timber	204	10		8	10	5
Stone	534	10		22	5	5
Plaster	40	10		1	13	4
Chert	93	10		3	17	6
Salt	17	10			14	7
Tiles	15	5			12	8½
Rails	47	0		1	19	2
Castings	74	0		3	1	8
Bones	20	0			16	8
Potatoes	41	0		1	14	2
	8260	0		344	3	4

SWARKESTONE LINE   FEBRUARY 1839

	Tons	Cwts		£	s.	d.
Corn	540	17	@ 9d	20	5	8
Sundries	1919	8		71	19	4
Clay	59	5		2	4	5
Tiles	39	15		1	9	11
Cast Rails	53	0		1	19	9
Plaster	268	5		10	1	2
Stone	241	0		15	15	9
Castings	46	10		1	14	10
Slates	32	0		1	4	0
Cement	520	10		19	10	4½
Bricks	80	0		3	0	0
Swine	22	2			16	6
Chert	58	0		2	3	6
Salt	17	10			13	1½
Iron	83	0		3	2	3
Lead	33	10		1	5	1½
Timber	15	0			11	3
	4209	12		157	17	1

LITTLE EATON LINE   FEBRUARY 1839

	Tons	Cwts			£	s.	d.
Stone	2463	10	@	3d	30	15	10½
Sundries	199	0	@	17d	14	1	11
Corn	18	0	@	12d		18	6
Mr. Holden	1832	8	@	17d	119	6	3½
Mr. Ray	549	19			35	6	9
Mr. Wooley	967	10			53	16	7½
Denby Old Colliery	157	2			10	15	10
Mr. Bourne	71	14			5	0	0
	6252	13			270	0	0

Of all the goods carried on the canal, however, the most unusual was probably that reported in the Derby Mercury of 19th April 1826 when: "On Saturday last arrived in this town by canal; a fine Llama, a Kangaroo, a ram with four horns and a female goat with two young kids . . . . all of which had been picked up in the course of the voyage of the Blonde in the Sandwich Islands in the Autumn of 1824".

In addition to the various goods carried the canal also served passengers. For a number of years a Market Boat equipped with seats and a fireplace left Swarkestone every Friday morning to carry market people to Derby and returned again at the end of the day.

For a number of years the canal was a financial and commercial success but competition from a number of railway companies from the 1840's onwards forced the company to reduce its tolls. Attempts were also made to sell the canal to the Midland Railway but negotiations came to nothing and the Canal Company struggled on with decreasing tonnage being carried year by year. The Little Eaton Line was abandoned in 1935 and in 1937 the company proposed also to abandon the Sandiacre line, but failed owing to the objections of I.C.I. After an abortive attempt at restoration by the Midlands Branch of the Inland Waterways Association in the early 1960's the Derby Canal Company finally succeeded in abandoning the whole canal by warrant in 1964.

The Peak Forest Canal

The Peak Forest Canal is not truly a Derbyshire canal but it deserves some mention since it terminated at Bugsworth (renamed Buxworth) in the north west corner of the county.

Built primarily for the purpose of supplying lime and limestone from the 'Derbyshire Dome' to the industrial and agricultural areas of Derbyshire, Lancashire and Cheshire, it ran from a junction with the Ashton Canal at Dukinfield to Bugsworth where connecting tramways linked the canal with local limestone and gritstone quarries. There was also a short branch to Whaley Bridge.

The original idea for the construction of this canal came from the Ashton Canal Company and a number of the Ashton Canal's shareholders were involved in its promotion and financing. The driving force, however, came from Samuel Oldknow who was elected to the committee on 7th August 1974 and later became its chairman.

Oldknow was an enterprising businessman with extensive interests in the area. He had built a cotton mill at Mellor and intended to construct lime kilns at Marple to burn limestone brought there by canal using coal mined from his own local collieries. He was therefore determined that this project should succeed.

Parliamentary authority for the Peak Forest Canal was obtained in March 1794 and construction commenced almost immediately. Benjamin Outram was appointed as Engineer with Thomas Brown of Disley as his Superintendant of Works.

The original scheme proposed a route from Ashton Junction through Dukinfield, Hyde, Woodley, Romiley, Marple, Disley and Bugsworth to a terminus at Chapel Middleton. From here a tramway was to be laid to Dove Holes. The plan envisaged two sets of locks, one flight at Marple and the second at Whitehough, one mile east of Bugsworth, four

The Bugsworth Basin

tunnels on the line of the canal and one on the line of the tramway, an inclined plane east of Chapel-en-le-Frith and numerous company wharves and warehouses.

At a meeting held in July 1795, in order to save money, it was decided that the canal should terminate at Bugsworth and the route from here to Chapel Middleton be covered by tramroad. Despite this saving, however, the company faced financial problems which hindered construction. Members of the committee had to lend money to the company in order to complete the summit level of the canal and the tramroad which was opened from 'the lime works' via Bugsworth to Marple on 31st August 1796.

Construction was completed by 1801 except for the flight of locks at Marple. Until further capital could be raised a steep single-track rope operated tramway was built which operated from the end of 1798 until late 1805.

The village of Bugsworth in Derbyshire played an important role in the operation of the canal and a massive complex of wharves, warehouses, stables and lime kilns grew up here. Limestone was quarried at Doveholes and other smaller quarries and transported by horse-drawn tramway to the canal at Bugsworth where it was loaded directly to narrow boats or converted into lime in the kilns which were built there. Trade grew rapidly. In 1808, 50,000 tons of limestone came down the tramroad, in 1824 the company loaded 291 narrow boats in one period of four weeks, and in 1833 was carrying an average of 1,743 tons and loading 279 boats weekly.

Many of the boats which operated on the canal were built and repaired at the boat building yard and dry dock which Oldknow had established on the top level of the canal close to the lime kilns. The boats built here had a carrying capacity of 25 tons each and were given names such as 'Buxton', 'Farmer', 'John Bull', 'The Duke' and 'Willersley Castle'.

The opening of the Macclesfield Canal and the Cromford and High Peak Railway in 1831 brought increased traffic on to the Peak Forest Canal and the dividend paid rose from £2 in 1827 to £3-10s (£3.50) in 1832 and reached a peak of £5 between 1835 and 1837.

In April 1843, however, "close competition with Railways and other lines of Communication" was reported. Tolls had to be reduced in order to retain traffic and dividends fell.

In 1846 the canal was taken over by the Manchester, Sheffield and Lincolnshire Railway on a perpetual lease. The same railway also leased the Ashton and Macclesfield canals. The three were jointly administered and usually known as the

Canal warehouse at Whaley Bridge (built about 1832)

A.P.W. A considerable volume of traffic was carried for many years especially in limestone through Bugsworth.

In 1833, however, the canal company was dissolved and the canal and tramroad vested in the railway company. By the turn of the century it had greatly declined from its heyday and in 1905 carried only 136,148 tons at an average toll of 4.6d per ton. The tramroad ceased operation in 1922 and the Bugsworth Basin was dewatered in the 1930's.

Further decline occurred after nationalisation and in 1948 and in the mid 1950's coal traffic from Stoke-on-Trent finally ceased after the closure of Goyt Mill at Marple.

Today the upper level is popular with pleasure craft from the Macclesfield Canal and restoration work is being undertaken at Buxworth.

Five Family Jaunts

1. — Explore the 18th Century Inland Port of Shardlow

The village of Shardlow is approached along the A.6. It is about twenty minutes drive from the centre of Derby and ten minutes from junction 24 of the M1.

Shardlow has been described as ". . . a textbook example of an original canal village" and "the best surviving example of the kind of 18th century inland port which blossomed during the Canal Age".

To explore Shardlow park your car at the public car park in Wilne Lane. Walk down Wilne Lane as far as the bridge over the canal. Turn left before the bridge and descend to the canal towpath; opposite is the New Inn (built as a beer house around 1777) and the Malt Shovel Inn originally the house of the manager of the adjoining malt warehouse).

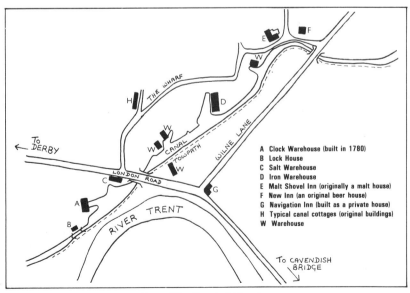

A   Clock Warehouse (built in 1780)
B   Lock House
C   Salt Warehouse
D   Iron Warehouse
E   Malt Shovel Inn (originally a malt house)
F   New Inn (an original beer house)
G   Navigation Inn (built as a private house)
H   Typical canal cottages (original buildings)
W   Warehouse

Map of the Canal at Shardlow

Turn left and follow the towpath towards the London Road Bridge. You will pass a number of interesting warehouses built in the 18th century as well as a cast iron milepost and a wooden crane used for loading and unloading goods from the barges.

Pass under the bridge and walk as far as Shardlow Lock. You may be lucky enough to see a boat passing through. On your return pause to look at the Clock Warehouse (now converted into a restaurant).

Leave the towpath at the London Road Bridge and return via 'The Wharf'. You will pass a row of 18th century canal workers' cottages and the rear of many warehouses. A few minutes later the path takes you back to the Malt Shovel Inn and the bridge leading to Wilne Lane.

If you have more time to spare, you could take a trip on a modern narrow boat or enjoy a meal at one of the many local pubs. Altenatively, if you would like to explore the village more thoroughly the best guide is an inexpensive leaflet produced jointly by Derbyshire County Council and the Arkwright Society. Entitled "Canal — Shardlow" it is available from various bookshops and tourist information centres throughout the county.

2. — Ride a horse-drawn narrow boat along the Cromford Canal

The trip boat 'John Grey'

43

This trip is ideal for a Summer Saturday or Sunday afternoon. A horse drawn passenger boat leaves Cromford Wharf at two o'clock and four o'clock on Saturdays, Sundays and Bank Holidays from April to September.

The 1½ mile journey takes you through pleasant countryside as far as the Leawood Pumphouse. This was built in 1849 to pump water to the canal from the River Derwent below. It was restored by volunteers and is now steamed during the Summer.

Walk on a little further over the Wigwell Aqueduct spanning the River Derwent as far as a cottage on the opposite side of the canal bank. Here you will see the start of the Nightingale Arm of the canal, built in 1802 to serve Peter Nightingale's lead works at Lea Bridge. The cottage was used by the canal lengthman.

On your way back (either by boat or on foot) look out for various buildings associated with the Cromford and High Peak Railway (wharf shed, office and workshops) which linked the Cromford Canal with the Peak Forest Canal. Approaching Cromford Wharf the buildings ahead of you to the left are a warehouse and counting house built by the Cromford Canal Company in 1794. The larger warehouse to the right was built in the 1820's by Nathaniel Wheatcroft, one of the principal canal carriers.

There is much else to see in Cromford, including Arkwright's Mill just across the road from the wharf. An excellent village trail is produced by the Arkwright Society.

All enquiries about the Cromford Canal should be addressed to:
The General Manager
Cromford Canal Society Limited, Old Wharf, Mill Lane,
Cromford, Matlock, Derbyshire
Telephone: Wirksworth (062982) 3727

3. — Learn about local waterways at the Nottingham Canal Museum

This trip may be squeezed in between shopping or combined with a towpath walk or a boat trip to make a half day out.

Nottingham Canal Museum from the rear

Located on the ground floor of a former canal warehouse, built and used by Fellows Morton and Clayton Ltd., the site includes loading areas and wharves. The displays are based on the history of the River Trent, canal and river transport, bridges, floods and archaeology of the Trent Valley over 6,000 years.

The two major exhibits are the ex-Fellows, Morton and Clayton motor boat 'Ferret' and the butty boat 'Ilkeston'. There is also much information, including photographs, maps and documents, about the Trent and Loughborough navigations and the Cromford, Erewash, Grantham, Derby and Nutbrook canals. Another interesting section deals with the wildlife found around our canals. The display includes coot, herring gull, heron, kingfisher, mallard duck, moor hen, mute swan, frog, toad and water vole. Other exhibits include narrow boat tillers, navigation lamps, traditional canal ware and a superb diorama showing what canals looked like and how they were operated in their heyday.

A small museum shop sells a variety of souvenirs and the old offices and stables of the Fellows Morton and Clayton Company next to the museum have been converted into a pub — "The Fellows Morton and Clayton Brewhouse Company, where you can see ale being brewed and "Joshers Fish Restaurant". (The slow horse-drawn barges which operated on the canal were known as 'Ordinary Joshers').

During the Summer the "Maid of Sherwood" operates 1 hour canal trips from the museum wharf on Sundays and Bank Holidays. If, however, you would prefer a stroll along the towpath of the Nottingham and Beeston Canal an interesting and informative canal trail may be purchased from the museum shop.

The Canal Museum is located on Canal Street, Nottingham almost opposite the Broadmarsh Bus Station on the A453, between the railway station and the castle. Admission is free and it is open at the following times:

> *Easter — October*
> Wed — Sat 10 - 12, 1 - 5
> Sunday 1- 5
>
> *October — Easter*
> Wed, Thur, Sat 10 - 12, 1- 5
> Sunday 1 - 5

All enquiries should be addressed to:
The Curator
Nottingham Industrial Museum, Courtyard Buildings,
Wollaton Park, Nottingham NG8 2AE
Telephone: Nottingham (0602) 284602

4. — Walk the towpath of the Erewash Canal from Sandiacre to Long Eaton

This is a very interesting walk which takes you past many buildings and engineering features associated with our industrial past.

Start your walk at Canal Street in Sandiacre. This leads directly to the towpath of the Erewash Canal. Looking down the towpath to the right you will see Springfield Mill. This is a lace factory built in 1888 by Terah Hooley. Between the

Springfield Mills at Sandiacre

factory and the canal you can see the engine and boiler house as well as a tall octagonal red brick chimney.

You should turn left away from Springfield Mill, keeping the canal on your right. After passing under Sandiacre Bridge and the A52 you will come to the junction with the now filled-in Derby Canal. The first few yards of the Derby Canal are in water as far as the stone-built arch bridge, only one parapet of which remains.

Just after this junction is Sandiacre Lock with lock and toll cottage. The toll house on the junction side of the cottage was used by the Derby Canal Company until 1832 when they built their own lock house (now demolished) on the opposite bank of the Derby Canal.

Carry on walking past the next lock (Duckholme Lock) and you will come eventually to the outskirts of Long Eaton. On the opposite bank of the canal are a number of early 20th century lace mills.

Just before you pass under the A453 Birmingham — Nottingham Road you will come to a particularly impressive mill building with a massive 110ft high circular chimney. This is Bridge Mill, a lace factory built in 1902 for Long Eaton Bridge Mills Co. Ltd. and now in multiple occupation. This is also an appropriate point to turn back though you may, if you wish, carry on as far as the junction with the River Trent about two miles further on.

On your way back keep your eyes open for wildlife such as ducks, moorhen and water vole. How many different types of wild flower can you see? Water lilies, woody nightshade, tufted vetch, bindweed, ragwort and willow-herb are all found in abundance but there are many more and it would probably be worthwhile carrying an identifcation book with you.

The complete walk should take about two hours. If you would like to try similar walks a number of books of towpath walks have been published and are available from local booksellers. One of the best in the author's opinion, is 'Canal Walks — Vol. 1 Derbyshire and Nottinghamshire' by John Merrill.

5. — Visit the Waterways Museum at Stoke Bruerne

This excursion takes you a little further afield but the Waterways Museum at Stoke Bruerne is well worth a visit.

Standing beside the Grand Union Canal, and housed in what was once a grain warehouse, this museum gives an intriguing insight into every aspect of canal life and history. On the ground floor beneath the dark wooden beams of the ceiling visitors are introduced to many of the themes of canal history, the transition from horse power to steam and then diesel, the colourful traditions and the hard grind of daily life. Exhibits include a traditional narrow boat cabin, a boat horse and a number of engines. On the first floor the emphasis is on the engineers who planned the canals, the navvies who built them, and the boat people and their craft who worked them. Costumes, painted ware, ropework and surveying equipment are among the many fascinating items on display. Finally, on the top floor, the displays concentrate on canal structures (locks aqueducts etc.) and on maintenance work. Many of the

The Waterways Museum and canal side cottages at Stoke Bruerne

tools used in everyday maintenance are on show together with a fire engine and a diving suit!

In addition to the museum there is much else to see and do at Stoke Bruerne. The adjacent museum shop stocks a wide range of literature on the canals of Britain. There are also lots of lively posters, illustrations to frame and drawings to colour as well as hand painted miniatures, traditional canalware, models to make and badges to wear. Outside you will be able to watch boats going through the lock and walk up the towpath to the entrance of the Blisworth Tunnel, the longest tunnel still in use on the waterways system. If you have time you can also take a short boat trip on the canal. For refreshment the Boat Inn and the Butty Restaurant face the museum on the opposite side of the canal.

The museum is open daily from 10.00 to 5.30 between Easter and October and daily except Mondays from 10.00 to 4.00 during the winter months.

To get there leave the M1 at junction 15 and drive 3½ miles south along the A508. A right turn about one mile beyond Roade brings you to the village of Stoke Bruerne.

All enquiries should be addressed to:

The Manager/Curator
Waterways Museum
Stoke Bruerne near Towcester, Northamptonshire
Telephone: Northampton (0604) 862229

BIBLIOGRAPHY

Primary Sources

In carrying out research for this book I made use of a wide range of primary sources including maps, plans, canal company minutes, pamphlets, tonnage accounts, parliamentary records and newspapers. These documents are held in a number of different depositories including local libraries, Derbyshire Record Office, the House of Lords Record Office and the Public Record Office.

Secondary Sources

'A Look at Shardlow's Past' — John Heath, Paddock Publications 1978

'Canals of the East Midlands' — Charles Hadfield, David & Charles 1966

'Canals of North West England' — Charles Hadfield, David & Charles 1970

'Derbyshire Industrial Archaeology: A Gazetteer of Sites — Part 1' — Dudley Fowkes (Ed.), Derbyshire Archaeological Society, 1984

'Derbyshire Industrial Archaeology: A Gazetteer of Sites — Part 2' — Dudley Fowkes (Ed.), Derbyshire Archaeological Society, 1986

'Industrial Archaeology of Derbyshire' — Frank Nixon, David Charles, 1969

'Industrial Archaeology of the Peak District' — Helen Harris, David & Charles, 1971

'Lost Canals and Waterways of Britain' — Ronald Russell, Sphere Books, 1983

'The Chesterfield Canal; notes for schools' — M. Mansell, 1968

'The Cromford Canal' — Cromford Canal Society, 1983

'The Cromford Canal Company' — J. W. Walker, Cromford Canal Society 1981

'The Derby Canal' — Michael Smith, Morley's, 1980

'The Illustrated History of Derbyshire' — John Heath, Barracuda Books, 1982

'The Leawood Pump' — Cromford Canal Society, 1983

'The Little Eaton Gangway' — David Ripley, Oakwood Press, 1973

'The Nutbrook Canal : Derbyshire' — Peter Stevenson, David & Charles 1970

'The Trent and Mersey Canal' — Jean Lindsay, David & Charles, 1979

'Transformation of a Valley' — Brian Cooper, Heinemann, 1983

INDEX

Other Related Titles

'Work and Play' *by Alan Bower*
features old postcards of the Nutbrook and
Peak Forest Canals

"Derby Old and New' *by Frank Rodgers*
features the Derby Canal in 1905 and 1874

'Derbyshire Characters for Young People'
by Elizabeth Eisenberg
includes a profile on James Brindley